PLANTS BE

CW00847726

Ayşegül Yıldırım is a poet and academic from Turkey. She has completed her PhD in Sociology at Goldsmiths, University of London. Her recent work has been featured in the anthology *Cornish Modern Poetries* released by Broken Sleep Books.

ISBN: 978-1-915079-47-3

Cover designed by Aaron Kent

Edited & Typeset by Aaron Kent

Broken Sleep Books Ltd
Rhydwen
Talgarreg
Ceredigion
SA44 4HB

Broken Sleep Books Ltd
Fair View
St Georges Road
Cornwall
PL26 7YH

Contents

Plants Beyond Desire

Ayşegül Yıldırım

opening: (a-)sexual conundrum[1]

it
is a
plant-tale,
plant-take-on-things,
plant-plan,
plant-becoming,
becoming-plant,
plantation,
plant-body,
plants who do not *heal*,
who do not *enchant*,
who do not exhale.
plants who do not blush or open,
plants who do not have
the concept
of going to work in the morning,
plants who cannot help but work,
deceptive plants,
imperceptible plants,
very visible plants;
the subject matter here and now.
even those who have no occupation
but drink water.

tree rules are grafted onto root exce(r)ptions.

---

1   After *Prelude* by Syvia Legris.

Tragicologic of plants

Fact: the difference between those who have nothing to say but have branches and those who live undersoil but have written poetry cannot be understood in current spacetime. Hints: the act of dreaming about, cooking and forbidding the branches at the same time.

The causes of branch growth: not open-access.

The plant audience: they do not hear or their hearing is not mainstream yet. Apparently they only touch.

We're in the final act yet we don't know - those who *know* the secret of branches always think there's a missing ingredient.

All branches are graceful liars.

mixed herbs

in your Italian food
some used to be
toxic operators
plants
used to conspire
some store
more ammunition
in the vaults
some doesn't enjoy
Mozart
some have
tooth sensitivity
but the gun
appeared long ago
in any case
there will be exogamy imposed
by the
extraterrestrial
human explosion
in molar and molecular
space-sense

familiarity Equisetum

things that are
stored in the memory of the
200-million-year-old horsetail
are not only about the
200-million-year-old horsetail.
And they don't mind.

The unexpected sound

came from the squeezed but
not dead. how many times can you
kill a plant? how many
times can you kill
A
plant? the root of the
core of the root
of the core
the seed the DNA
the infinitesimal
do not make the church bell ring for death.
it's only the
B
side of the latest member.
the parish where growing and the interstice
are not despite each other.
within the *in*audibility range
(the whole universe) –
respond, respond, respond,
embrace, embrace (exist) and
wake up. An
infinite song of the
non-calculation abundance.

provisionary plant anxiety

I live in the dark for years
sometimes, followed by
a flood before a draught thatshakesme
from top to toe. I understand
there's a crisis. I shut myself up.
Perhaps it's already
dark outsideIdon'tknowI don'tknow.
Shoes here. Feel my feet frozeninside
wherever they are.
Can't.Shoesneveroff. Mightescape.
SweatFlood.
shoes send me messages from below -
[...]
I know I can never afford sunshine, ever.

Metastasis of anthropocentrism

Is the Chamamaedorea in my room mad at me or my shadow or their shadow? Or do they have shadows? Are their shadows their own image? Is it still shadow when you can't see? Do they have demons? Are their demons their own image? Do they have ambitions? Are their ambitions leaf-shaped and do they at least have similarity to their shadows? Does it have any relation to the demon? Do they mirror their senses in mine? Is that the neuro-botanics of our existential bond? Do they speak English? Can I make them speak English? I think I like her. Is she going to leave me now?

Unity

Plants never follow their
dreams. There is no soil-made desire.
       The body responds to sensory
       stimula, to beginnings
       and endings immediately.
       Except of its own
       beginnings and endings.   There is *none*.

                                                In *sense*.

The ultimate synch is in between
the tip of the fingers and the surface
where the universe begins.
The plant talks and never loses.   For it doesn't know.
The politician would recover if they knew.

I like plants, so they like me

the obsession and the talent to analyse
lies behind the difference between
the desire for plants and

plants.

house plants / office plants / plants that like the sunshine
/ and those who don't / plants that clean the air /
Feng-shui plants / shopping mall plants /
supermarket plants / plants for Capricorns / Valentine's
Day plants / tropical plants / plants that don't resemble
anything. which one would you like?

the desire of the world as reflected onto the plant, reflected
back to the universe. here, raining, please have it all.
competition of dissatisfaction. I'm grabbing a cactus for my
desk. they've traveled here on their own. the 200-million-year-
old perennial is grinning, still doesn't mind. despite those in
the vicinity who want their body.

uproot

Her only childhood memory about plants is picking up flowers.

Dahlias from grandmother's garden; a tiny medley of purple dead nettles, camomiles, vervains brought home from park visits with mum.

By the end of the day, they'd always be in the rubbish bin. Years later, she got put in a tiny medley of humans packed in an aeroplane, never to come back. Those left behind are still tired from grief, even though the plane has not crashed yet.

By the time the purple on the hands were cleared, dead nettles flourished. Nobody had cried for them ever. Later, the idea of home has gone for us all, tiny corruptions magnified. Except for the roots.

re-root

Someone told me to burn sage indoors but the true magic is
that no two leaves are identical. And the fact that I took a
dry leaf from where it waits for me in the mud. It was the
beginning of winter in Falmouth and sometimes you
need that moment of acknowledgement of your
image by the assemblage of the holy cliff.
I'm not able to speak their language.
I was receding endlessly. The leaf stayed
with me nevertheless. He just fell down,
he thinks. But he only had to leave
himself gently to the ground.
No two fallings are
identical. Some-
times you need
to root faster
than you can
fall.

correspondence

When
she saw the weeds growing from
the interstices of the garden wall,
she was crying over the poisons
of her father over the phone. Their
eyes met. She told him about the plants.
He didn't sound interested.
His heart, a solid structure in a jungle,
beautifully covered by ivies feeding
on tears. They all must
have been blushed by this time of year.

Hello

Thank you for buying me
peonies. Otherwise I'd think
my female body is worthless
and that you won't offer me anything
for doing unpaid household chores.
Now everything's complete. I'd rather
be algae in my next life, swimming
eternally in the ocean, part of the
moss community that doesn't
excite anyone;
or a medusa, hair made
of seaweed which can escape
the life on earth.

Sending snakes xx

depression diabetes

Psychiatry is modern agriculture:

unify	homogenise
stigmatise	categorise
analyse	dissect
prescribe	pestify
make efficient	make efficient
make efficient	make efficient
make efficient	make efficient
make efficient	make efficient
make efficient	make efficient

grapes are sweetly poisonous,
poisonously
sweet too,
everyday
life.

the flow of the thoughts

The
    rustling
          of
            the
              leaves.   Something's lost.

An involuntary response to the winds.

[More tickling than the sound of the
ink-dipped roots on the page. My
roots. Then]

A breakdown when the
uncontrolled desire is about to
collide   The car stops.
Rustling on both sides of the
road. Creases on the page, pierced.
I used to cross   Creeks on the path.
without a single toxic bag. I whistle.
Trees look away, same always. Lights
off from the heart. Fasten   Lights off.
the seatbelt tight. The apartment
flats far away, still as tiny as
Bachelard described.   I arrive,
the night still relies on black
bleeding roots.
As if they can save me from my own

bog.

Analysis of a snake plant (questionnaire)

Q: Do you feel offended by being called a snake?

A: A snake wouldn't touch me, so the answer is no. But even if it did, I know it doesn't have the capacity to destroy all other beings.

Q: Where are you from? Do you miss your home?

A: I'm already home.

Q: Do you really need little water?

A: I don't like to have water everyday. But it depends on other things too such as warmth.

Q: Do you enjoy living in your current place?

A: I don't know what you mean.

Q: What do you dream of?

A: Light and dark are the two facets of the same thing.

Q: Do you get sad?

A: If I'm really struggling to keep myself going as I am, I'm already a different being, too open to other organisms to be hosted in and around me. They're not always nice.

Q: What does water taste like?

A: Myself.

Q: Can you actually see?

A: Senses are the compartmentalised version of an undifferentiated unity. I am acutely aware of the variations in my environment. You can't *see* my *responses*.

Q: You grew up without a family. Do you feel the absence of it?

A: I don't know what you mean by *absence*.

Q: Do you learn a language?

A: Language is a new preconception. I only know how to make gestures.

Q: Do you like the people around you?

A: I'd rather have them like each other as it's safer. I think they're in trouble. They're only home in the evening and they gaze into a blue light.

Q: I think we will need to repeat the interview. Don't you enjoy to be interviewed?

A: It's interesting to get to know you. The questions told me very much about you. But my answers will not mean anything to you. At least for a long time.

The gap

Provence, lavender fields. It
was summer when I graduated. Sweetheart
██████████, this is surreal, I thought, stroking
the heads of the purple community. ██████████
██████████
I rushed to Wilko and got a bottle of lavender
essential oil. As I smelled the drops on my pillow,
someone stroked my head, congratulating. A bliss
from the stalks followed by the super
machinic harvest. Flying hats in the sky. Only the
tunnel vision of purple dust afterwards. The bottle
reads Provence.
The lavender ██████ feel this
much.

ripe

avocadoes   most

                  visible
                  when
we have

mouths
                  visible
                  as

lips when
you're in

love
                  visible
                  when

getting married

                  visible
                  as
ropes
                  when

it ends
                  visible
                  when
you sit and

write it.

Plants, I'm down

[despite us and the planet, a plant and becoming-plants are never lonely.
They derive their function from what they're connected to. A
plant is air-soil-water-lightness to us. A cult dedicated to
function. The fact of this made me exhausted. Over the years,
my roof got stolen, I was locked *in*, the water was cut, a lot of
the trees died. It was a thousand-year journey. Here I am. and
I *need* more and more of the plants.]

Statement From the Plants That Were the Upper-Middle Class Décor of A Proust Novel

We can't comprehend the fact
that the act
of giving one part
of the world
that lives at
some level
to another part
of the world that
lives at another
level,
or sometimes at the same level,
or sometimes at overlapping levels
in variable ways,
is explained with
love.
We never saw that
worked.

The next statement
will be about
fragrances. Merci.

red roses

perhaps not.
if they
were to see the colour of themselves,
their responses and
how they'd deal with it
would have been determined by their
neighbours who
have such colours and who do not
and whose silent flesh is
acknowledged and sacred
the most.
not
by love.

Plant plenitude too
ends where
eyes form and
start
reflecting.

Acknowledgements

The ultimate motivation to write this book and submit it to Broken Sleep Books came from encouragement from Aaron Kent when he responded to one of my poems. Thanks to him for being incredibly supportive of poets and for believing in the present work. I am very grateful to all members of the Broken Sleep team for their efforts to support this book from the selection process to publication. Thank you also to the Broken Sleep authors who showed enthusiasm about the book since the reveal of the title and the cover. You are a great community which I am proud to be part of.

Endless gratitude to my partner and my mother.

PLANT YOUR UNREST

Milton Keynes UK
Ingram Content Group UK Ltd.
UKHW011833100624
443885UK00004B/162